# T.U.R.N. O.N. T.H.E. S.W.I.T.C.H!

Written by

Carla Joan O'Reilly

◆ FriesenPress

Suite 300 - 990 Fort St
Victoria, BC, V8V 3K2
Canada

www.friesenpress.com

ISBN
978-1-5255-4630-3 (Hardcover)
978-1-5255-4631-0 (Paperback)
978-1-5255-4632-7 (eBook)

*1. SELF-HELP, DEPRESSION*

Distributed to the trade by The Ingram Book Company

# T.U.R.N. O.N. T.H.E. S.W.I.T.C.H!

Are you ready for change?

# Are you ready to
# T.U.R.N. O.N. T.H.E. S.W.I.T.C.H?

T.U.R.N. ON. T.H.E. S.W.I.T.C.H! is for anyone ready for a change.

There are points in everyone's life when they may go through a personal struggle or adversity. Sometimes you may hit a wall, get in a rut, or fall down a hole. Those are nice and easy ways to describe battling severe depression. However, when you are actually dealing with it, the real thoughts and feelings can be catastrophic and without hope. I am talking about being suicidal.

My name is Carla O'Reilly. I am an author, inspirational speaker, and mental health advocate. I also came very close to being a suicide statistic.

I am here today because I made a choice to help others, and for the past ten years, my life has been transforming because of the powerful tools from T.U.R.N. O.N. T.H.E. S.W.I.T.C.H! I took steps to heal, sometimes small and sometimes big, but most importantly, I took the steps. I decided I was ready to grow and change, and that I had something to contribute on this earth.

I suffered for four years with debilitating postpartum psychosis and obsessive compulsive disorder, and it nearly ended my life. My breakthrough came when my friend, Tania, forcefully and purposely sold me on finding the will to live. She encouraged me to be a fighter. I made the choice to fight my way out of the illness, and I found my calling to help others. This became my purpose for living.

If you are struggling, and are open and ready for a change, this book is for you.

I am here to share the simple, powerful, and easy tools from T.U.R.N. O.N. T.H.E. S.W.I.T.C.H! that will help you transform your life.

Anyone can read this book and apply the tools to their life. If you are open and ready and willing to change, you will see just how powerful the tools can become.

I am a true believer that you can accomplish any goal you set your mind to. This book is an example of the power of belief in helping others.

I want you to start by closing your eyes, and snapping your fingers. Every time you snap your fingers, I want you to say: TURN ON THE SWITCH! TURN ON THE SWITCH! TURN ON THE SWITCH! REPEAT IT THREE TIMES! You will start to feel peaceful, powerful, and confident.

This is just the beginning! When you make the choice to T.U.R.N. O.N. T.H.E S.W.I.T.C.H! and use the tools, there are no limits to what you can achieve. There is no dream, too big or too small, that cannot be realized.

# T.U.R.N. O.N. T.H.E. S.W.I.T.C.H!

## The Healing Transformation

When you begin your healing journey, you must follow a few rules.

The first rule is to keep an open mind.

There are many ways to heal. Just as we are all unique, there are some healing methods that will resonate and work for us, and some that won't.

Try multiple ways of healing. Included in this book are many types of alternative healing therapies.

The second rule is that healing is a marathon, not a sprint. Healing has no time or space relation or measure. Healing is infinite. People are often afraid to heal because they assume they will need to relive the trauma.

The third rule is that healing should be loving. The act of healing should allow you to feel at peace. As you begin your journey, remember this is a gift for you. This act is all about you and it is time to learn through joy. If you have experienced something traumatic or if you are overcoming an adversity, this next experience should bring you peace. I don't believe in reliving trauma. If you are living in the past, how do you expect to move forward? Periods of our life have to be put to rest in order to grow. Eventually, in order to start living explosively, you must say, "it is what it is, and that was in the past."

The fourth rule regarding healing is to open the door to endless opportunities.

When I set out to begin my healing journey, I had decided I was going to try anything I could get my hands on in order to heal. There are limitless types of alternative healing therapies available: Angel Therapy, Reiki, energy work, tapping, oils, meditation, affirmations, light therapy, to name a few. My biggest piece of advice: Keep it simple. If it does not feel relaxing or has too many rules or steps, than this can be overwhelming for someone who is struggling with depression or trying to overcome an adversity, which will make it difficult to stay motivated.

Have you heard of Angel Therapy? If you ever get the chance, I highly recommend it. Each sessions is extremely powerful and therapeutic. If you are looking for loving guidance in your life, Angel Therapy is definitely the place to start.

Below is my recollection of my first Angel Therapy session. We began with a card reading, which was followed by a Circle of Excellence meditation. Anyone can and should use this meditation (contact me at www.thesmilingmask.com and I can create one for you). I suggest trying this, and finding an Angel Therapist who is right for you. You can also purchase Angel Therapy cards. The cards are an uplifting way for you to connect with loving thoughts and ideas.

My angel therapy appointment was set for 1:00 p.m. Upon arrival, I felt instantly relaxed. I entered a room filled with angels statues, crystals, and the scent of frankincense. I felt ethereal and at peace. There was a sound of a fountain running. My Angel Therapist's name was Ariel, and she invited me to sit down. She pulled out her first deck of Angel cards. "How are you, my child, and what is it that you need to know?" Close your eyes and meditate for a moment," she said.

I took a deep breath. "I want to know what my purpose is. Am I on the right path?"

"I will ask the angels; let us see what the cards reveal." She pulled out the golden cards and laid four out in front of me. She flipped over the first card. "High Priestess Cleopatra," she said, and looked at me knowingly. "You were a high priestess in a past life. You are a leader and have much wisdom to bestow. Be careful whom you trust; only share your advice with those worthy."

The second card was flipped. "Master Marksman Diane," she said. "Oh, very interesting. Focus your intention—you will make your mark. This means that you should only devote your time to things that are in your sacred circle. Your time, energy, and ideas are of intrinsic value. Use them wisely."

The third card flipped. "Sorceress Dali Lakshmi. Your future is bright. Worry will get you nowhere. Let the golden sun shine in your life."

The fourth card was flipped. "Ocean Keeper of the sea, Mya. The doors of your true calling are opening for you. There is a golden opportunity. Walk through them."

Ariel smiled. "Now are you ready to enter the golden circle?"

She stood behind me and laid a white sash on my shoulders and around my neck. "Now we must both begin to meditate and take deep breaths. When you hear the chime three times, you will enter your circle."

Our breathing became rhythmic, and all my thoughts and fears were washed away. I felt as though I was beginning to leave my body and heading towards a light. Then I heard the chimes: One, two, three.

I found myself standing in front of a door, and a voice whispered, "come inside."

I looked and saw three angels. They held open a white robe. The room was filled with gold, gold everywhere, and there was a marble platform in the middle of the room. They covered me in the robe and guided me to the platform. They placed a crown on my head. They spoke in unison.

"This is your circle. This is your place of power. Whenever you need us, we are with you. You can enter this circle at any time. Just place your thumb and your middle finger together. All your strength, all your courage, all your power, all your mentors, all your coaches, and all your balcony people are here for you. They are surrounding you with love. All of your accomplishments, all your steps forward. Remember your power, and you will bring forth electrical, explosive change."

I felt as though I was falling back to earth. I knew my purpose, and I knew my intention. I was like a star ready to explode.

The three chimes brought me back to earth. My session was over.

At the end of the reading, she said some very important things to me.

"We all have jobs to do. We are put here on this earth with a purpose, and each one of us is given a task. What you went through was terrifying, painful, and horrific. However, you survived in order to help others. You are very strong, powerful, and driven. You will help so many people and save lives. You have a gift to motivate others to see their personal power. Always take time to quiet your mind when you need wisdom. Ask, and it shall be given.

Teach others how to choose their thoughts; teach others how to change them to positive; teach others how to find a passion and obsess about it."

My angel therapy session had opened the door to receiving wisdom. I knew I had been given a powerful gift to help others.

After supper, I decided to go for a walk in the rain. The sky was filled with lighting, and I could hear the powerful thunder. I went and sat on a park bench to watch the storm. I remembered the Angel therapist saying that sometimes, if we quiet our mind, we will hear the answer.

The wind brushed my hair. I heard the thunder crackle. I saw the lighting flash. I closed my eyes and then I heard it. "T.U.R.N. O.N. T.H.E. S.W.I.T.C.H!" the voice called to me. "T.U.R.N. O.N. T.H.E. S.W.I.T.C.H! You have the power to T.U.R.N. O.N. T.H.E. S.W.I.T.C.H!"

And then, just like that, the fifteen wellness tools materialized and poured out of me like raindrops on paper.

# T.U.R.N. O.N. T.H.E. S.W.I.T.C.H!

Find a passion and obsess about
it. Together, we will make the
world a better place.

**T**urn on the switch! Choose your thoughts and change to positive!

**U**se your imagination. Create and visualize your success.

**R**ecognize the power of your thoughts. Positive energy is invigorating!

**N**urture your mind, body, and spirit continually by doing activities that you love.

**O**pen your mind to endless opportunities. Set S.M.A.R.T. goals and achieve them.

**N**ever underestimate the power of your strengths. Find out what they are, and use them.

**T**he truth will set you free. When you are struggling, the most important thing to do is ask for help and talk about your feelings. Use your voice and destroy the shame. You will begin healing quicker.

**H**elp others. We have two hands: one to help ourselves and one to help someone else.

**E**xercise every day, and deep belly breathe. Get active! This is so therapeutic, and you will feel amazing.

**S**elf-awareness, acceptance, forgiveness, and love—use these simple tools from **Behind the Mask** to unlock the key to wellness.

**W**rite you story; rewrite your story. Try something completely different and be the star of your life.

**I**nspiration is everywhere. Find a passion and obsess about it. You will help make the world a more amazing place.

**T**ake time to laugh each and every day. Laugh out loud, and even better, laugh with a friend. Laugh at yourself. Don't take yourself too seriously.

**C**onfidence comes from within. Compliments are fabulous. Supercharge your self-talk and see what you can accomplish.

**H**eroes, mentors, coaches, and balcony people—find them, listen and learn from their wisdom. Balcony people cheer your every victory, and will carry you when you need assistance. Support is all around you.

# T.U.R.N. O.N. T.H.E. S.W.I.T.C.H!
## Tool #1

## Tool #1: Gratitude

Do you want to know how to T.U.R.N. O.N. T.H.E. S.W.I.T.C.H?

Of course you do! That is why you have picked up this book. You have decided that enough is enough. You are finally ready for change. This book is filled with simple, effective tools that will transform your life.

I am a firm believer that baby steps are the most successful way to change your life positively. It's a known fact that it takes twenty-one days to form a habit, and if you are using the tools from T.U.R.N. O.N. T.H.E. S.W.I.T.C.H! I assure you that positive things will start happening in all areas of your life (physical, emotional, and spiritual).

I am going to share the tools with you in subsequent chapters. But remember, the first and most important tool is:

*Gratitude.*

Gratitude will change your life. I want you to start by looking down at this book and thanking yourself (or whomever purchased it for you) for the opportunity to transform your life. Take a moment to sit still and say "thank you" over and over. How do you feel? This is a practice of blessing your higher self, the spirit in you that is open and ready for more abundance and for living a joy-filled life!

If you only remember one thing from this book, remember the power of gratitude.

Every day is a gift. Every breath that we take is a gift. Before you jump out of bed, make a list of everything that you are grateful for.

*I have a great job. I have healthy food to eat. I have a beautiful house. I have family and friends whom I love. My children are healthy and a gift in my life.*

Make a list of all the things you love.

This first tool is so simple. You only have two types of thoughts: positive thoughts and negative thoughts. Gratitude is the most effective way to wake up your positive thoughts and get them multiplying! There will be no room for your negative thoughts!

Make your gratitude list a daily habit. You will see your life transform.

You always have the power to choose your thoughts. *Choose positive.*

As a survivor of postpartum psychosis who battled mental illness for four years, this habit has been life-changing for me. Learning to count my blessings brought me out of a dark hole. Every day was an opportunity for more joy.

Gratitude helped shape and transform me from a person who suffered with mental illness to an author and advocate with a dream to raise awareness. Ten years ago, I followed my dream to write a book to help other mothers suffering with postpartum depression, along with two other amazing, powerful women named Elita Paterson and Tania Bird. Together, we co-authored *The Smiling Mask: Truths about Postpartum Depression and Parenthood.* Visit www.thesmilingmask.com for more information about our project and legacy.

Our mission was to provide awareness, acceptance, and understanding of postpartum difficulties, and to provide hope, healing, and harmony for families.

This project was based on the value of gratitude, with every step we conceived and then achieved.

There was a circle of gratitude flowing from:

- Each of the team members and our families who supported our project.

- Our publisher, Peggy Collins, our book cover and website designer, Jay Roach, and our filmmaker, Dianne Oullette.

- The many supporters in our communities who came to hear our stories of hope.

- All those in our circle of survivors who suffered in silence and were ready to use their voices and begin their healing journey.

With each book that was read and shared, there will be thousands of healing circles created, and gratitude will be shared and spread.

Gratitude and love helped create T.U.R.N .O.N. T.H.E. S.W.I.T.C.H! I have made it my passion to inspire and help others, and the balcony people in my life encouraged me to follow my dream to write this book.

Gratitude is a habit you have to exercise, and the more you do it, the stronger you will be. Just imagine how amazing the world would be if we were all practicing gratitude. Start now! Ask yourself, *what are you grateful for?*

Make a top ten list of all the things you're grateful for. Trust me: You will begin to feel amazing.

# T.U.R.N. O.N. T.H.E. S.W.I.T.C.H!
## Tool #2

## Tool #2: Use your imagination. Create and visualize your success.

As a child, I was told to dream big. Many of us were. "Use your imagination," they said. "Be creative!" Once I became an adult, I thought this had to stop.

I was wrong. You never have to stop dreaming. Whatever success or happiness looks like, visualize it.

Before I get ready to inspire audiences, I always set the intention that my message is going to help someone in the audience. My words are going to jolt them into action.

What are you passionate about? What gets you excited? What gets you out of bed in the morning? A famous quote is "Find something you love to do, and you will never work a day in your life!" This is very true.

Take a look at your core values and interests, and spend time doing activities accordingly. Maybe you have been working in a dead-end job, unappreciated and not using your valuable skills. Now is the time to build on your passions. Sometimes you have to do something outrageous.

When I began the Smiling Mask project, I was working in a dead-end job, going through a divorce, and in the process of losing my house. But I knew that I needed to leave all those negative energies behind in order to embark on my healing journey. I quit my job, said goodbye to my spouse, and packed up my house (I was about to lose everything)—but what I gained was *freedom*.

I used my dreams and visualizations to create a new, stronger, more powerful version of myself. I lost eighty pounds and became an author and public speaker at conferences across Canada. I knew this was something I was meant to do.

So I challenge you to use visualizations, and to dream in colour. Take time every day to dream those big dreams. Sit and write down what you want to do with your life—and then *see it*.

What have you got to lose? You may even write a book—or two!

# T.U.R.N. O.N. T.H.E. S.W.I.T.C.H!
## Tool #3

## Tool #3: Recognize the power of your thoughts.

Your thoughts are powerful. As someone who battles Obsessive Compulsive Disorder, I had to learn to control my negative thoughts, or they would overpower my life. Through self-education, I learned that I not only had the power to control my thoughts, but that I could *choose* what I thought. That was a breakthrough moment.

I also learned that chronically complaining about what was going wrong in my life was a choice as well, and being negative was exhausting. Have you ever spent time with a Debbie Downer, or an emotional vampire? They can suck the life right out of you with all their complaints. Pay attention to how you feel when you spend time with them. Are you uplifted and ready to take on the world? Or are you left feeling drained?

You only have so much energy. Use it wisely, and focus on the positive. Use your energy to bring happiness and abundance into your life and the lives of others.

To deal with the Debbie Downers in your life, be upfront and tell them that they need to put an end to their griping.

Tell them that they need to T.U.R.N. O.N. T.H.E. S.W.I.T.C.H! and buy a copy of this book. If you invest in yourself, you are more likely to be dedicated to making changes. The old adage is so true: *You can lead a horse to water, but you can't make it drink.*

Tell them you just read about me, and my simple tools changed your life. Tell them you look forward to getting together in three weeks to share gratitude lists.

Become a positive promoter, in your workplace, at home, with family, and with friends. People will want to be around you. And guess what? You will be making the world a more positive place.

# T.U.R.N. O.N. T.H.E. S.W.I.T.C.H!
## Tool #4

## Tool #4: Nurture your mind, body, and spirit.

When you make the choice to heal, you need to think of yourself as multi-dimensional. You need to heal your mind, body, and spirit. This is why using only medications for treatment with mental illness is not always effective. You have to treat the whole body and get to the heart of your pain.

So start by researching different ways to nurture yourself with self-care. Decide which methods make you feel happy. We are not all the same. Some will love hard-core exercise, and others will find joy in yoga.

This tool is so important. Have you ever heard the phrase, "If you don't take care of yourself, you won't be able to take care of anyone else"? Be selfish and practice self-care. Recognize when you need a break, and also establish boundaries. You don't get a special prize for taking on the world. So stop being a martyr.

When you T.U.R.N. O.N. T.H.E. S.W.I.T.C.H! and nurture you mind, body, and spirit, you take time for yourself and engage in activities that make you feel alive and happy.

You exercise; you eat healthy; you get plenty of rest; you read a good book; you watch a funny movie; you enjoy a good meal.

For some daredevils, this may mean going skydiving or bungee jumping. For the less adventurous (like me), this may take the form of walking, or dancing, or going for a massage, or meditating.

Make a list of some activities you like to do, and set up a daily, weekly, or monthly schedule to devote time to yourself. Observe how you feel. Instead of being run down or worn out, you will feel invigorated and have extra energy for whatever comes your way.

I am a big believer in small steps to great success. When I came out of my depression, I started to eat healthy and walk daily. I lost eighty pounds over a period of one year. Exercise doesn't need to be complicated, but rather dedicated. This is something I fit into my life daily, and I have maintained my weight loss for ten years.

I use the 80/20 rule for healthy eating. This works! Eighty percent of the time, I eat healthy. And twenty percent of the time, I eat whatever the hell I want! You don't feel deprived or cheated, and you are able to maintain your weight loss.

# T.U.R.N. O.N. T.H.E. S.W.I.T.C.H!
## Tool #5

## Tool #5: Open your mind to endless opportunities, and set S.M.A.R.T. goals.

Whatever your dream is, you have to be open to it. There are endless opportunities available to you. Never put a limit on your potential.

Whatever that dream is, you can achieve it by setting

S.M.A.R.T. goals. S.M.A.R.T. is an acronym for goals that are specific, measurable, attainable, realistic, and timely.

Whenever I have to start a project, I break it down into smaller steps to complete it.

Here is a breakdown of how I used S.M.A.R.T. goals to lose weight:

I made the goal **specific**. *I want to lose eighty pounds.*

I made the goal **measurable** and **attainable.** *Every week, I would like to lose two to three pounds, which is a healthy pace for weight loss.* I will achieve this goal by walking three times per week along with weight training and eating healthy.

I made the goal **realistic** and **timely.** *I will lose eighty pounds in one year.*

Did you reach your goal this week? Start a meal plan and keep a food diary. Begin an exercise program and measure your progress, whether you're focusing on weights, cardio, or running.

Track your achievements. How far could you run when you started out? How much farther can you run each day, each week, each month?

Is your goal **realistic**? Yes! You can and will do anything you set your mind to. A goal of one to two pounds per weeks is a healthy weight loss that is maintainable.

Is this goal **attainable**? The point here is to make it realizable. The way you do this is by breaking down your goal into smaller goals.

Ultimately, the most important part of goal setting is **ACTION.** You can write all the goals you want, but taking the first step, and then continuing to forge ahead with one foot in front of the other, is the most important.

Just like writing this book. I set smart goals to achieve my dream!

When you write down your goals, you are held accountable to them. Putting your thoughts on paper make them real. When we started the Smiling Mask project, we wrote down all of our goals. When we looked back at that list ten years later, we achieved everything we said we would, and more.

Be very mindful to only share your goals with balcony people. Others may try to squash your goals and dreams. Don't listen to them. I had many people tell me that I could not write a book or engage in public speaking. I have written three books and spoken over two hundred times across Canada. My purpose and passion to raise awareness overrode my fear of failure.

One of my favorite quotes is by Walt Disney, who said, "If you can dream it, you can do it."

# T.U.R.N. O.N. T.H.E. S.W.I.T.C.H!
## Tool #6

## Tool #6: Never underestimate your strengths.

The doctors told me I would have Obsessive Compulsive Disorder for the rest of my life. But they never said how I had to use it. Being obsessive is one of my God-given strengths, along with the ability to turn thoughts into actions.

T.U.R.N. O.N .T.H.E S.W.I.T.C.H! is all about finding a passion and obsessing about it. You will make the world a better place. When you obsess about positive things, you have no choice but to attract amazing things and people into your life.

My choice to no longer be a victim to postpartum psychosis and to help other mothers by co-authoring *The Smiling Mask* was spiritually driven, and was driven to save families.

We had a team with a dream, a belief, and a persistent passion to destroy the stigma of PPD and to help families.

*The Smiling Mask* was written in forty weeks, released in 2008. We called it the birthing of our second baby. In 2009, we released *The Smiling Mask* documentary.

In 2011, we released our sequel, *Behind the Mask: Trust, Adjust, and Transform your Life!*

I have an amazing team, who loved to brainstorm, put thoughts into action, and motivate others to see their personal power.

Do you know what your strengths are? If you know what they are, or are in a career that is using them, I am excited for you! If you are still searching, don't feel bad: You are not alone.

In my early twenties, I spent a few years writing for a newspaper because I loved it, and it never seemed like work. Readers would ask me where I got the ideas for my articles, but they just seemed to come to me. Writing has always been my passion, along with seeing others find their personal power, confidence, and success.

During my dark depression, I had no drive and no interest. I found myself in plenty of jobs that left me feeling exhausted, stuck, and depressed.

Here is what I have learned: We all have strengths and gifts. Take some time to search out what yours are. When you are doing things that come easily and effortless to you, guess what? You will be able to do them quicker and faster, and you will enjoy going to work.

So maybe it is time to do some research, take a personality test, try a new career, or start with a hobby that can become a career.

# T.U.R.N. O.N. T.H.E. S.W.I.T.C.H!
## Tool #7

## Tool #7: The truth will set you free.

My belief is that we are all actors in a play, and we choose which stories (dramas, romances, comedies, etc.) we are going to play in. It's my belief, and you can take it or leave it. Beliefs are just ways of making sense of how strange life can be. The first act of my personal play was quite tragic, but thankfully, I realized you can be the hero of your own story, and you have the power to change your circumstances.

Nothing could have prepared me for my journey into motherhood, or my battle with postpartum psychosis. The only way out sometimes is *through*. I had to go through it to come out the other side as a changed person, who was stronger, more powerful, and compassionate about mental health. I was never the same; the lenses through which I viewed life had changed.

At first I was a victim: I was angry, I was low, and I had nothing to live for. Fortunately, my saving grace and my light in the world was my son, Cam. I knew I had to keep battling for him. I could not imagine how he could grow up without me. He was my touchstone and my reason for living. I learned that I needed to speak my truth, and that lesson was the most healing, the most powerful, and the most transformative.

When you are struggling with depression, the most important thing you can do is *ask for help*, and talk about your feelings. Use your voice and destroy the shame. You will begin healing much quicker.

After a four-year-long battle with postpartum Obsessive Compulsive Disorder and psychosis, I finally made a courageous choice to join a PPD support group. I remember being scared and nervous because I was going to be sharing my secrets with complete strangers. This day turned out to be one of the best days of my life. I met my best friend Tania. Our friendship would be lifelong, and would be the impetus for the dream of the Smiling Mask project along with our other co-author and kindred spirit, Elita. I often think that if I had never gone through this, than I would never have met my best friends, and we would never have written *The Smiling Mask*. Suffering with PPD would still be shameful and stigmatized.

The support group was amazingly therapeutic, and I am a big promoter and believer in its healing power. The day I started to get better was when I released all those secrets I had been carrying for so long, and I stepped into that sacred circle.

I met some amazing women who changed my life forever, and our bond is so strong because we have shared the same pain. And we also healed together.

I have learned that talking about any problem, secret, or struggle is the answer. When you open yourself up and surrender the shame, you allow healing to begin. Seeking counselling or joining a support group has immediate benefits in healing. You will also be helping others and, in turn, be helping yourself.

# T.U.R.N. O.N. T.H.E. S.W.I.T.C.H!
## Tool #8

## Tool # 8: Help Others. We have two hands: one to help ourselves and one to help someone else.

Helping others has been the foundation for my own healing. One of my mentors told me, "Your gift is to help others. You have survived this experience so you can be an inspiration to others. Use your voice and share your story." I took this to heart and began speaking about my experience as a psychosis survivor.

I began mentoring mothers across Canada, and now globally, ten years ago. I knew that if I could save one life, it would be worth it. And I witnessed beautiful healing all around me as mothers came forward to share their stories. I am also grateful for the strong friendships I have forged with women I have met who are survivors. Our paths crossed for a reason, and we have a sacred connection. The shame and sadness that once consumed us all was now replaced with empathy and hope to help others.

Take this opportunity to find a passion that helps others. Then donate to it, volunteer for it, or pay it forward.

Complete a good deed without telling anyone. When you are helping, you have less time to worry about your own problems.

Do you have a friend, family member, or co-worker who could use some support? When you take time to help out others, you will feel enriched and purposeful. Start with your inner circle, your close friends and family. Ask yourself if there is someone really struggling who could use a listening ear. Maybe they need a hug. Make a list of people who could use your help.

The simple act of helping is like skipping a stone in the river, causing a ripple effect. I believe we are all here to make the world a better place. Start small. Mother Theresa said that peace begins with a smile, so smile at everyone you meet. You will feel amazing, and so will they.

# T.U.R.N. O.N. T.H.E. S.W.I.T.C.H!
## Tool #9

## Tool #9: Exercise every day, and deep belly breath.

Exercise is good medicine for mental health. Get Active!

This is very therapeutic, and you will feel amazing.

During my depression, I stopped exercising and eating healthy.

This caused me to spiral downwards, deeper and deeper. I was in that deep, dark hole for nearly four years.

When I became well again, the first thing I started to do was go for walks.

I would walk for just twenty minutes every day. Eventually, I started running for fun. I felt amazing.

When you are struggling with a stressful situation or decision, or when you are experiencing negative thoughts, going for a brisk walk can help to clear your mind and release endorphins.

Try it! Small steps lead to success. My success was making an effort each and every day to be physically active, whether it was walking, cleaning, or shovelling.

Everyone is different. So take time to do something you love. Maybe it is a sport, dancing, yoga, or running. I tried Zumba and it was fun (but disastrous!). I decided to stick with walking and running.

Do something active three times a week, and watch how amazing you will feel.

When I made the decision to get healthy again, I took it upon myself to eat healthy, but would still leave room for guilty pleasures— the 80/20 rule. I lost eighty pounds in one year, and ten years later, I have never looked back. I learned to view food as fuel for my body, and to eat things that made me feel better. Unfortunately, I had to give up fast food, which made me feel awful and lethargic. I do enjoy the occasional fry, which I steal from my son on rare occasions. We all love fries!

# T.U.R.N. O.N. T.H.E. S.W.I.T.C.H!
## Tool #10

## Tool #10: Self-awareness, acceptance, forgiveness, and love.

These are the tools from *Behind the Mask: Trust, Adjust, and Transform your Life*, our wellness workbook and sequel to *The Smiling Mask*. You can use these tools to unlock the door to wellness. But first you will have to ask yourself, *am I ready to transform?* Sit and ponder this for a moment. Ask yourself if you're ready to be the most profound version of yourself. Change can be uncomfortable; some people won't like the new you. Some of your friends and family won't be able to handle the sparkle—but that's their business and none of yours.

These tools are vital, in terms of your ability to move forward in your healing. This will be that defining moment where you have to say, "It is what it is, and I will be more than what happened to me." You will need to look for the lessons in whatever trials you endured, and see the strengths that those experiences empowered you with.

This is when you'll transform from victim to victor.

If you are struggling with depression, loss, divorce, or overcoming adversity, check out our sequel *Behind the Mask*. This is a wellness workbook with which you will work at your own pace to begin your healing journey. Remember, healing is marathon, not a sprint. Everyone heals in their own time. "Just when the caterpillar thought the world was over, it became a butterfly!" the old proverb goes. This will be a metamorphosis, and you will have many epiphanies. You will change and you will grow.

This is a four step process with multiple levels in between, and you are always going back and forth, but moving to a higher level of peace with each step forward.

The first step is to become self-aware. What are your beliefs? Are they serving you, or are they holding you back? Have you experienced anything traumatic or painful in your past? Are you ready to release it?

These exercises will stretch you, and you will never be the same. You will be stronger and more powerful!

The second step is self-acceptance I had to do a lot of work in order to heal. I struggled for many years with self-acceptance. I finally learned that we are all beautiful and unique. I had to embrace who I was: the good, the bad, and the ugly.

If we were all the same, wouldn't the world be a boring place? So indulge yourself. Be as sparkly, as crazy, and as original as you can be every day.

Accept who you are, with no apologies. Be extraordinary! My friend nicknamed me Blingy and told me, "You always look so sparkly, no matter where you go!" I took this as a huge compliment. I treat getting ready as a sport because when I look good, I feel good. I have accepted that I love to take pride in who I am and how I look—this is my spirit shining outwardly.

The third step is forgiveness. This step is crucial in your healing transformation. You can't move forward if you can't get over the past.

In order to heal, I had to forgive myself and others for things that had happened in the past. They say that holding a grudge is like grasping a hot coal with the intent of throwing it at someone else; You are the one who gets burned.

So here is what I suggest: Think of forgiveness as a gift you give to yourself. This is so powerful. This has nothing to do with the other person or event. This is all about your peace. You also don't need to let that person know. This is all about you.

Here is a powerful affirmation to use (I will talk about affirmations a little later). Start by closing your eyes. Get quiet and take ten breaths in and ten breaths out. Focus on your breathing, and then say the words: *I forgive you, I forgive me, and I set myself free!*

Say it again with me now: *I forgive you, I forgive me, and I set myself free!*

How do you feel? At peace? Was there a release? You can also picture a dove flying away with your pain and hurt. Eventually, after doing this exercise and a lot of reflection from the workbook, you should begin to feel neutral about the experience. When this happens, you will know you are in a place of forgiveness.

Who is someone you need to forgive? Write it down, and make this a goal to work on.

Maybe you need to forgive yourself.

The fourth step is self-love. This is where you bring in all the tools that you have learned so far, and surround yourself and others in love. When self-love occurs, helping others is a natural by-product. You help others not out of obligation or duty, but from your heart's center.

In order to get to the core of loving yourself, try some affirmations. Observe for a few days the things you say to yourself. Are they loving? Create some new powerful affirmations that are all about loving who and what you are. Don't make this complicated. Try using the following affirmation: *I love you, I am loving, I am lovable.* The most beautiful words you can hear will eventually transform your spirit.

Remember, you come to believe the things you tell yourself, and the types of things you tell yourself are habit forming, so repeat your affirmations every day. Just imagine how amazing you will feel when you come to a place of self-awareness, acceptance, forgiveness, and love. This will be ethereal and heavenly, and it will give you the opportunity to share your true, powerful self with others. T.U.R.N. O.N. T.H.E. S.W.I.T.C.H! and let your beautiful light shine through.

# T.U.R.N. O.N. T.H.E. S.W.I.T.C.H!
## Tool #11

## Tool #11: Write your story; rewrite your story. Try something completely different, and be the star of your own life.

Journaling is one of the quickest ways to start your healing. In fact, I started to write *The Smiling Mask* only months after my son was born. Writing is therapeutic. Take time every day to write about what you love and what you are grateful for. This can take the form of a list of goals, a bucket list, or a gratitude journal.

So how has your life been so far? Have you struggled with feeling inadequate, always standing in the shadows or feeling like you don't matter?

I give you permission right now to be the star of your own life.

Feel it! Own it! Invite it!

You are a star.

We only get one chance; this is not a dress rehearsal. I challenge you to wake up tomorrow and act like a star. Actually feel it. The world is your oyster, and good things are happening all around you. There are miracles happening every day, and you deserve them.

When asked the question, *who are you?* I used to say, "I am a monster, a freak, I am a horrible mother. I have postpartum psychosis."

Now I stand proud and say, "I am Carla O'Reilly, author, inspirational speaker, and mental health advocate. I am creating global positive change and creating a legacy for my son."

Remember to let your light shine bright and look the part. My grandma taught me that when you look good, you feel good. I embraced this belief. I never saw her unmade; she always had her face done and wore a fancy suit. I admired that about her, and she explained that her love for fashion and dressing was her self-care armour.

She told me a story about being hired as a dress shop manager. Her boss stopped her one day and said, "Who do you dress for?"

She replied in her strong, self -assured way, "I dress for myself." I loved this proud self-proclamation.

Dress for yourself, and always dress for a party! This is my motto. I purposely wear clothes and jewellery that makes me feel strong and confident.

One of my passions as a motivational speaker is to look and dress professionally. I turned my passion for jewellery into another opportunity to earn an income and became a jeweller with Fifth Avenue Collection (www.fifthavenuecollection.com/coreilly). I advertise my product every day by wearing it, and the quality is amazing.

Start using your strengths. Be the star. Always dress for the party. And T.U.R.N. O.N. T.H.E. S.W.I.T.C.H!

# T.U.R.N. O.N. T.H.E. S.W.I.T.C.H!
## Tool #12

## Tool #12: Inspiration is everywhere. Find a passion and obsess about it. You will make the world a better place.

This is where you should start asking yourself, *what makes me happy? What do I love?* Focus on it!

Working as a mental health advocate, and motivating and educating for the last ten years, has been an amazing experience.

My passion to help others made the work invested seem easy and effortless.

Any free time I had, I devoted to helping others and raising awareness on postpartum depression. This was my passion, and I did it while working and raising my son. People thought I was crazy when we announced we were writing *The Smiling Mask*, but it was the people who said "go for it!" that we listened to, and we never looked back.

Perseverance is my middle name, and never giving up became my game.

I put one foot in front of the other, and no matter how big or small, I kept taking steps to grow. That was the key to T.U.R.N.I.N.G. O.N. T.H.E. S.W.I.T.C.H! and finally writing this book.

Motivating others has been so healing, powerful, rewarding, and mind blowing. I loved seeing positive change in others. Having spoken over two hundred times, I have witnessed healing transformations occur when the shame and sadness of mothers was finally destroyed. This has been my gift, and I feel grateful to have been part of that moment.

Harvey Mckay said, "Find something you love to do, and you will never work a day in your life!"

When you find a passion and you are working to help others, your life will be truly blessed.

So step back and make a list; what are some things that you love to do?

Follow your dreams and go for it. What have you got to lose? There are no failures, only learning moments. Every step is a step forward!

# T.U.R.N. O.N. T.H.E. S.W.I.T.C.H!
## Tool #13

## Tool #13: Take time to laugh each and every day. Laugh out loud, laugh with a friend, laugh at yourself, and don't take life so seriously.

T.U.R.N. O.N. T.H.E. S.W.I.T.C.H! with laughter! Remind yourself that life is too short, and ask yourself, *will this matter in a year?* Most things aren't worth getting your panties in a knot over. Unfortunately, I had to learn this lesson the hard way as I was a chronic worrier. A friend gave me a good piece of advice: "You just have to go with the flow and become an observer." If someone is trying to push your buttons, sit back and understand that they likely have some underlining issues to deal with that have nothing to do with you. At the end of the day, you just have to laugh about it.

Throughout my journey, humour has been my saving grace. Even in my darkest hour, I knew there was hope if I could still laugh. I use laughter daily. I love to sing, dance, be crazy, and have fun.

I like to joke about my vanity and that I am a Libra. If you have done any research on your birth month, there can be some truth in it. Libras love balance and are said to be very vain. I make fun of myself and my obsession with sparkle. My friends call me the sparkle queen.

So if you ever get the opportunity to hear me speak, you will see me make fun of myself and incorporate my laughter tool.

I show the audience what I look like first thing in the morning. This can be quite scary. I am real and have no makeup on!

Then I hold up the famous Nick Nolte mug shot, in which he looks like he has been hit and dragged by a bus—that is pretty much how I look first thing in the morning. Google that picture and see if there are any similarities!

Life can be so serious, whether it's because you are battling with mental health or because of all those tough things that pop up in life to test your sanity. Using humour as a way to cope is the best advice I can ever give. Find the humour in being human. Make time to be with people who make your laugh, and who accept you and love all your quirks and crazy traits.

One of the most life-changing events for me was to fall in love with someone who loved my laugh—My partner, actually encouraged my laugh. He said, "You have a great laugh. Very unique and genuine." From that wisdom, I have learned to take time to be more silly, goofy, and funny.

The moral of this tool is to spend time with people who love your laugh!

Life will be splendid, fantastic, and never dull.

# T.U.R.N. O.N. T.H.E. S.W.I.T.C.H!
## Tool #14

## Tool #14: Confidence comes from within. Compliments are fabulous. Supercharge your self-talk and see what you can accomplish.

Have you ever noticed how wonderful you feel when someone gives you a compliment? Well, my motto is *Don't wait for someone to tell you how amazing you are; tell yourself every day!*

In order to remain positive, you need to recognize your self-talk. Self-talk is what you say to yourself on a regular basis, based on years of self-sabotaging beliefs. They can be things from your childhood, from family, friends, and spouses. A huge part of T.U.R.N.I.N.G O.N. T.H.E. S.W.I.T.C.H! is learning to destroy the beliefs that aren't serving you and to change your self-talk to positive.

During my dark days, I had very negative self-talk. My friends opened up my eyes to the power of positive self-affirmations. What you say internally about yourself becomes what you believe. Beliefs can be positive or negative. They can be ugly things that were said to you as a child. You may have carried these limiting voices for years. They can mold you and shape you, and stop you from becoming strong and powerful. Are you ready to own your personal power? Get ready to build yourself up with affirmations.

When I began my healing journey, I took a good look at my self-talk. Wow! No wonder I was struggling with shame and sadness. No wonder I had trouble getting out of bed in the morning. I would never think of speaking to another human being the way I had been speaking to myself. I would say things to myself like, *you are stupid, worthless, dumb, dirty, fat, ugly.* . . . But today, these are just old tapes that I have discarded from my mind.

Make it an exercise to throw those tapes of negative self-talk out. Get rid of them. Burn them. Make it a ceremony!

And get ready for the new tapes.

Now I start my day with *you are beautiful, powerful, amazing! You are a woman who is making positive change for mothers and families.*

This is habit forming. Start everyday by looking in the mirror and saying three to five affirmations. Start with *Good morning, beautiful!*

No matter what you may be struggling with—whether it is relationships, body image, confidence, work success, wealth, or health—your thoughts become your actions, and by thinking positive, you will attract more positive into your life. T.U.R.N. O.N. T.H.E. S.W.I.T.C.H! and turn on those powerful affirmations. You will transform, inside and out.

# T.U.R.N. O.N. T.H.E. S.W.I.T.C.H!
## Tool #15

## Tool #15: Heroes, mentors, coaches, balcony People: Find them, and listen and learn from their wisdom. Balcony people will cheer your every victory and will carry you when you need support.

Every great star needs a coach. If you wish to succeed in any endeavour, take a moment to look around at who you are spending time with. Are they lifting you up? When they hear your ideas, are they encouraging you to go for it? Oprah said, "Surround yourself only with people who are going to lift you higher. Life is already filled with those who want to bring you down."

Balcony people are those special spirits in your life who lift you up and make you feel powerful. Balcony people are not afraid of your success. They will cheer your every victory and will hold your hand when you need support.

Who do you admire? There are so many heroes in the world. Take time to make a list of who you want to follow. Read up on them and their stories. I bet you will find out that they started out as ordinary, but had a dream to be extraordinary.

I don't believe in accidents. I think everything happens for the greater good.

I thank God every day that fate brought Elita Paterson and Tania Bird into my life. They taught me how to heal, forgive myself, learn to use my voice, and believe in my gift to write and speak to empower others.

They taught me to believe in and love my unique strengths and talents.

When we connected, we put magic put into motion. We sparked a healing wave of education, empowerment, encouragement, and empathy. With each idea we had, we cheered; our belief was that there was nothing we couldn't do. The last ten years of my life have been an amazing adventure. I had so many wonderful experiences with these two special ladies: We attended so many wonderful conferences together and had wonderful trips across Canada. But it was the fun and laughter that I will never forget. And because we have shared traumatic experiences, we have an immense comfort level with one another.

When you T.U.R.N. O.N. T.H.E. S.W.I.T.C.H! and begin searching for balcony people, amazing things will happen. Look for friendships that will help you grow, learn, and allow you to be yourself. There are millions of amazing people in the world, following their passions and working to make the world a better place. Reach out, do some research, and find them. Find a hero. Make a list of your hero's past and present, and learn more about how they grew great. Cultivate relationships with mentors who will take you to higher levels. There is no limit, and you get to decide how far you want to go. Surround yourself with balcony people, and see that there are endless opportunities to what you can achieve.

Be the most powerful person you can become, a firecracker that explodes with inspiration. Be the light in a world of darkness, and shine bright for our children—they will need balcony people!

# Epilogue

If someone would have told me to look inside a crystal ball ten years ago, I could never have imagined how my life would have turned out, or where I would be today.

I followed the T.U.R.N. O.N. T.H.E. S.W.I.T.C.H! tools that I have laid out before you and never stopped dreaming. I am a great thinker, but I am even better at putting thoughts into action. This is the key: If you have a dream, go for it! No matter how long it takes or what the dream is, you can achieve it. I am living proof of that, and so is the book you are reading.

Now, I pose this challenge to *you*.

You have the power to T.U.R.N. O.N. T.H.E. S.W.I.T.C.H!!

You have the power to choose positive thoughts.

You have the power to transform your life.

Find a passion and obsess about it. Together, we will make the world a better place.

Whatever your dream is, big or small, T.U.R.N. O.N. T.H.E. S.W.I.T.C.H! and make these dreams a reality.

Give these tools as a gift to someone you love.

Remember to T.U.R.N. O.N. T.H.E. S.W.I.T.C.H! Everyday.

# T.U.R.N. O.N. T.H.E. S.W.I.T.C.H!

## Reflection Exercises

1. Create a bucket list! What are ten things you would like to do or accomplish?

2. Create a positive affirmation for yourself.

3.  What are some beliefs that are not serving you? These can be about yourself, your health, your finances, your relationships, etc. Write them down, and then work on destroying them with positive self-talk.

4.  Are there any events, people, or aspects of yourself that require your forgiveness to help you move forward towards happiness? Write down the areas that need forgiveness.

5.  Gratitude Journal: Write down six things that you are grateful for today.

# Dedication

This book is dedicated to some very important and influential souls in my circle of life.

To my parents: You have given me strong values and the gifts of courage, wisdom, and a drive to help others. You have been my cheerleaders throughout this journey, always encouraging me to follow my dreams to help others. I will never be able to measure the love you have given me. There will never be enough words to say how grateful I am for you.

To my sisters: You are always my lights at the end of a tunnel. You have always been my shoulders to cry on and have carried me when I needed you. I admire each of you for the gifts you possess: strength, kindness, loyalty and courage.

To my Handsome: You have shown me what strong love, respect, patience, acceptance, and kindness look like. I have learned so much from you. Your quiet wisdom is immense, and you always ground and protect me. You make me smile and laugh. You encourage me to speak my mind, and to be outrageous and sparkly! I can be who I am, with no apologies.

To my circle of friends (and you know who you are): You have given me so many gifts of kindness, love, and support. Each one of you is a warrior, a goddess, a queen, and an angel. Know always how precious you are to me. For you, I see wellness, abundance, and continued healing. Remember to always sparkle and shine!

To my son: You are my prince, and although you are young, you have a wisdom that is beyond your years. I see great things for you. Remember every step, big or small, is a step forward. Remember to always follow your dreams and use your natural strengths. Remember to believe in yourself, and if someone tells you that you're not good enough or you'll never make it, it's nothing but a golden opportunity to prove them wrong. Always know that I loved you from the moment you breathed life, and that I will never stop.

To all the mothers who have struggled with postpartum depression in the past, present, or future: My hope is that my story inspires you, and will lay a foundation for you to begin your own healing journey.

The future holds bountiful awareness and empathy for mental health. I encourage you to take hold of your power and T.U.R.N. O.N T.H.E. S.W.I.T.C.H!

# About the Author

**Carla O'Reilly**, is an award winning author, inspirational speaker and Mental Health Champion. She began her healing transformation when she co-authored *The Smiling Mask-Truths about Postpartum Depression and Parenthood* and *Behind the Mask-Trust, Adjust and Transform your Life!*. For nearly a decade she has been spreading a healing wave of education and empathy across Canada for maternal mental health awareness. Now she is ready to share her message of healing to the masses with the simple powerful tools that transformed her from surviving to thriving!

Visit me at
**www.thesmilingmask.com**
for more information about how I can
**T.U.R.N. O.N. T.H.E. S.W.I.T.C.H!**
at your next event and inspire your audience!

Printed in Canada